The Science of
Glass

Lesley Ward

T0027069

Contributing Author

Allison Duarte

Consultants

Jeffrey E. Post, Ph.D.
Chairman, Department of Mineral Sciences
Curator, National Gem and Mineral Collection
National Museum of Natural History

Stephanie Anastasopoulos, M.Ed.
TOSA, STREAM Integration
Solana Beach School District

Publishing Credits

Rachelle Cracchiolo, M.S.Ed., *Publisher*
Conni Medina, M.A.Ed., *Managing Editor*
Diana Kenney, M.A.Ed., NBCT, *Content Director*
Véronique Bos, *Creative Director*
Robin Erickson, *Art Director*
Michelle Jovin, M.A., *Associate Editor*
Mindy Duits, *Senior Graphic Designer*
Smithsonian Science Education Center

Image Credits: p.5 (bottom) Birkerts Building, The Corning Museum of Glass, United States, Corning, New York, photo courtesy of The Corning Museum of Glass, © Timothy Hursley; p.8 (top) PhotoStock-Israel/Alamy; p.8 (illustrations) Kevin Panter; p.9 (top) Shah Marai/AFP/Getty Images; p.10 DeAgostini/Getty Images; p.12 (bottom left) Courtesy of Salem Community College; p.13 (top), p.19 (top left), p.19 (bottom right), p.20 (right), p.21 (top right), p.22 (top right), p.25 (bottom right) © Smithsonian; p.13 (bottom) National Museum of Health and Medicine/Alan Hawk; p.18 (bottom) Jeff Whyte/Shutterstock; p.19 (top right) Collection Museum Prinsenhof, Delft; p.19 (bottom left) Wellcome Collection; p.21 (top left) © Estate of S.J. Woolf. Collection of the National Portrait Gallery, NPG.87.TC2; p.21 (bottom right), p.32 (left) Courtesy Kiva Ford; p.23 (left) Courtesy of the Corning Incorporated Department of Archives & Records Management, Corning, NY; p.23 (right) Collection of The Rakow Research Library, The Corning Museum of Glass, Corning, New York; p.24 (left) Collection of The Corning Museum of Glass, Corning, New York; p.24 (right) The Dianne Williams Collection on Pyrex, The Rakow Research Library, The Corning Museum of Glass, Corning, New York; p.25 (top left and right) Courtesy of the Corning Incorporated Department of Archives & Records Management, Corning, NY; p.25 (bottom left) Courtesy Corelle Brands LLC; p.26 (bottom) dpa picture alliance/Alamy; p.27 (center) age fotostock/Alamy; all other images from iStock and/or Shutterstock.

Library of Congress Cataloging-in-Publication Data

Names: Ward, Lesley, author.
Title: The science of glass / Lesley Ward.
Description: Huntington Beach, CA : Teacher Created Materials, Inc., [2019] | Includes index. | Audience: Grades 4 to 6. |
Identifiers: LCCN 2018018119 (print) | LCCN 2018019068 (ebook) | ISBN 9781493869565 (E-book) | ISBN 9781493867165 (pbk.)
Subjects: LCSH: Glass--Juvenile literature. | Scientific apparatus and instruments--Materials--Juvenile literature.
Classification: LCC TA450 (ebook) | LCC TA450 .W37 2019 (print) | DDC 620.1/44--dc23
LC record available at https://lccn.loc.gov/2018018119

☀ Smithsonian

Teacher Created Materials

5301 Oceanus Drive
Huntington Beach, CA 92649-1030
www.tcmpub.com

ISBN 978-1-4938-6716-5

© 2019 Teacher Created Materials, Inc.

Table of Contents

A Clear View through Glass

A researcher looks at human cells under a microscope. A scientist studies bacteria in a Petri (PEE-tree) dish. A student boils liquid in a test tube. What do these activities have in common? They all involve items made of glass. For centuries, glass has been **essential** to scientific exploration. Every laboratory in the world contains shelves of glassware.

Glass containers used for science come in all shapes and sizes. Scientists use beakers, bottles, and test tubes. They use flasks, funnels, and dishes. Each glass item has been carefully designed. Each one has a purpose. Test tubes are used to hold and mix liquids. Funnels help transfer liquids. Graduated cylinders precisely measure volumes.

A scientist looks through a microscope at a specimen in a Petri dish.

Glass is the perfect material for science containers. It is clear, so scientists can see what is inside. Most glass melts at high temperatures. But some glass is heat resistant. That means applying heat will not break it or change its shape. Glass will also not react with or affect most chemicals used in experiments.

The next time you grab a glass of water, take a second to observe the amazing material in your hand. Thanks to glass, scientists can do research that makes the world a better place!

New York's Corning Museum of Glass has the largest collection of glass in the world with more than 45,000 pieces.

obsidian

This Aztec arrowhead is made from obsidian.

black obsidian necklace

The Origins of Glass

Although the glass we use today is man-made, the earliest example of glass on Earth occurs naturally. It is called obsidian. Obsidian forms when volcanoes erupt. **Molten** rock in the form of lava pours out. When lava cools quickly, it sometimes hardens as this smooth glass. It is usually black or green. It is also **translucent**.

Obsidian can be found in rock formations around the world. There is a large amount of the shiny glass on the Obsidian Cliff in Wyoming. People can pick up chunks of it at the base of the tall, black cliff.

Throughout history, people have used obsidian for many purposes. American Indians used it to make weapons, such as knives and arrows. It was easily broken into shapes for blades or arrowheads. People in ancient Greece used obsidian for mirrors.

Obsidian has many modern uses too. Some medical instruments, such as scalpels, can be made of obsidian. They are even sharper than steel. Jewelry made from obsidian is popular too. Some people believe the glass has healing properties. They also think that obsidian brings good luck to a person who wears it!

SCIENCE

Molten Glass

Glass is made by melting together several minerals. The main ingredient is usually silica. Silica often comes in the form of sand. The minerals are mixed together and melted in a furnace. Temperatures can go as high as 1,700° Celsius (3,100° Fahrenheit). The solids liquefy and form molten glass. The **malleable** molten glass is removed from the furnace. Then, it is shaped and allowed to cool and harden.

Archaeologists have found evidence that people began making glass around 1600 BC. Tiny glass objects were found during archaeological digs. Ancient people heated sand to a molten state. Then, they put the liquid into **molds** to make whatever they needed, such as simple tools and jars.

The first glass **vessels** were made through core-forming. People covered a clay core by winding a coil of molten glass around it. After the glass cooled, the clay was scraped out, leaving a hollow vessel. The vessels were small but useful and could hold perfume, medicine, or anything else people wanted to store. People could store many items in their dwellings. Many people wanted these glass vessels for themselves.

This ancient Roman glass vessel is from the first century AD.

1 A core is formed out of clay.

2 A rod is inserted into the clay core.

3 A coil of molten glass is wrapped around the core.

4 Handles are shaped out of molten glass.

5 The clay is scraped out.

Molten glass has the thickness of **molasses** and is usually a bright orange color.

This modern illustration shows an ancient Egyptian glassblower.

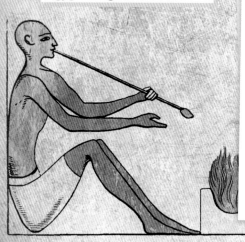

People in Syria invented the blowpipe around 300 BC. This simple tool revolutionized glassmaking. **Artisans** placed globs of glass that had been softened by the heat of a fire onto the ends of hollow pipes. Then, they blew into the pipes while they rotated them. The short puffs of air formed the glass into bubbles. This practice became known as glassblowing. Thanks to this technique, glassblowers could make vessels of any shape or size.

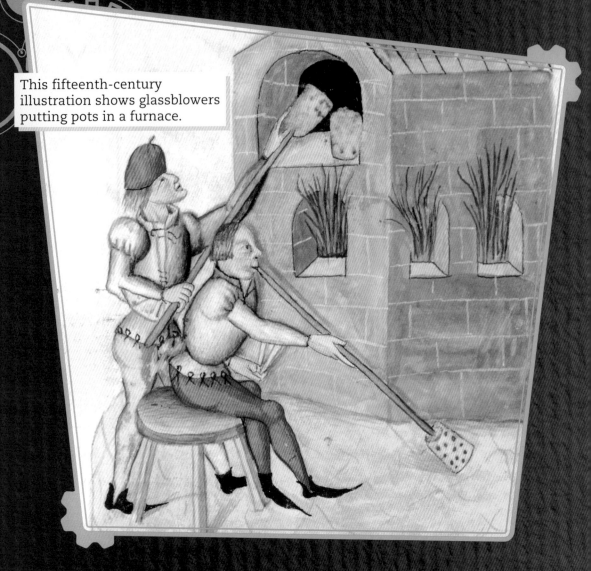

This fifteenth-century illustration shows glassblowers putting pots in a furnace.

People in Europe began making glass over a thousand years ago. Murano, an island near Venice, Italy, was the center of the glassmaking world. Glassblowers there became famous for their skills. They were treated like royalty.

Artisans were both artists and scientists. They experimented with glass. Sometimes, they added metal powders to molten glass. This created vibrant colors, such as violet and gold. Glass was a luxury at the time. It was expensive. Only rich people could afford things made of glass. Those things were usually made with yellow or green glass.

Then, in the mid-fifteenth century, a chemist in Venice named Angelo Barovier invented the process to make clear glass. The glass was called *cristallo*. He ground up quartz pebbles instead of using sand. His recipe and other methods were secret. Glassblowers could be put to death if they shared them!

Glassblowers in other countries learned from the Italians. Soon, glass spread around the world. British settlers built the first glass factory in the New World in 1607.

At the start of the twentieth century, a glassmaker invented the first automatic glassblowing machine. It could make 240 glass bottles a minute! Glass items were now cheaper to make. More people could afford to buy things made of glass.

cristallo vase

quartz pebbles

TECHNOLOGY

Fiery Furnaces

A glassblower uses three furnaces to heat glass. The first contains a crucible to hold the molten glass. A crucible is a container that can withstand high temperatures. In the second furnace, the glassblower reheats a piece of glass while working with it. The third furnace is used to slowly cool glass so it doesn't break. Ancient glassblowers relied on wood to fuel their fires, but today's furnaces often use gas.

11

Scientific Glassblowing

In the 1700s, scientific exploration was popular in Europe. People wanted to solve the mysteries of the universe. They sought knowledge. They studied physics and chemistry. They gazed at the night sky and learned about the stars.

These scientists gathered materials and ran tests on them. They realized containers were necessary for research. Sometimes, they had to store things. Other times, they wanted to boil liquids over flames. Glass was the ideal material to make these vessels.

A nineteenth-century scientist tests glass.

Scientists worked with glassblowers to design and make containers. If they couldn't find suitable containers for experiments, they designed them. Then, they asked glassblowers to make them. Some scientists learned how to blow glass so they could produce their own vessels!

A Salem Community College student melts glass.

The vessels came in many shapes. They looked like the beakers and test tubes used in labs today. Sometimes, scientists still ask glassblowers for help. But there is a problem—there are not many scientific glassblowers left. Salem Community College in New Jersey is trying to change this. Students at Salem can earn a degree in scientific glassmaking. Their classroom contains a row of glowing furnaces. These budding glassblowers study chemistry. They learn computer **drafting**. They design and make glass tools that are essential for important research.

A glassblower creates a
scientific instrument.

The First Microscope

Three Dutch men invented one of the
first microscopes in the 1500s. It was
made of several lenses connected by a
hollow cylinder, or tube. The top lens
that people looked through was the
eyepiece. The lens at the bottom was
an objective lens. Together, the lenses
made objects look about nine times
larger than they actually were.

By the early 1900s, people in Germany had perfected making glass using a mixture of chemicals called soda lime. That mixture was being used to make most of the world's laboratory glassware. This was a problem for many scientists during World War I. The Germans would not sell glass to their enemies, including the United States and Great Britain.

American scientists began making their own glass. It was called borosilicate. It was incredibly strong. It could withstand high temperatures. It could also hold **volatile** chemicals.

Borosilicate glass was more expensive to make than soda lime glass. But scientists liked its durability. Borosilicate glass spread in the scientific community. Today, it can be found in most labs around the world.

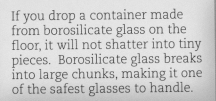

If you drop a container made from borosilicate glass on the floor, it will not shatter into tiny pieces. Borosilicate glass breaks into large chunks, making it one of the safest glasses to handle.

Glass and Scientific Exploration

Glass can be a perfect lab partner for scientists. Many experiments cannot be done without glass. Glass has many properties that make it suitable for science.

First, it is **nonporous**. It does not absorb or change most substances it touches. Second, glass is transparent. Scientists can see clearly through it. Glass can also be formed into different shapes. A scientist can design a glass container to fit an experiment. Some glass is made to be heat resistant. It won't melt when exposed to heat. It won't expand with heat either. It can withstand extremely high temperatures. Finally, glass can be reusable. A test tube can be cleaned and used again. When scientists are done with it, glass can be recycled. It is good for the environment.

A scientist prepares to heat a chemical in a glass beaker.

Different types of glass are used in scientific research. Some glass is made from quartz. Quartz is a mineral. Glass made from quartz is very strong. It is used to make jars and tubes used for experiments. It has also been used for windows on spacecraft.

Another type of glass is actinic glass. It is dark brown or amber in color. It protects materials that are sensitive to light. Fritted glass is also used. This glass is porous. Gas or liquid can pass through it. Fritted glass is used to filter solid **particles** from liquids. Some scientists use siliconized glass. This type of glass has been treated to stop material from sticking to it. This makes cleaning up after an experiment easy.

Sometimes, scientists need new types of glass to solve problems. So, they invent their own! For example, nuclear radiation causes most glass to turn brown. This was a problem in nuclear experiments. Scientists developed a glass that doesn't turn brown. This glass has been used for observation windows in nuclear reactor plants.

Scientists at the Corning Glass Works laboratory in New York invented photochromic glass in the 1960s. *Photochromic* means that something changes color in response to light. Photochromic glass contains tiny crystals. These crystals clump together when light hits them. This glass is used in eyeglasses to make them turn dark in the sun.

actinic glass jar

quartz crystals

Night-vision goggles often have lenses made out of chalcogenide (KAL-kuh-juh-nahyd) glass. This glass transmits infrared light that is not normally visible.

This space shuttle's windows are made of strong quartz glass.

A Variety of Vessels

People use the many different types of glass to make scientific instruments. One of the most common instruments is the test tube. It is a long, narrow container made of thin glass. It is used to heat and store liquids. Beakers are larger containers that can stand on their own. They have wide openings and small spouts for pouring. Funnels are pipes with wide necks and narrow stems. They are used to channel liquids into vessels with small openings. Flasks have large bases and small necks. Substances are often heated in flasks. A Fleaker® is a combination of a flask and a beaker!

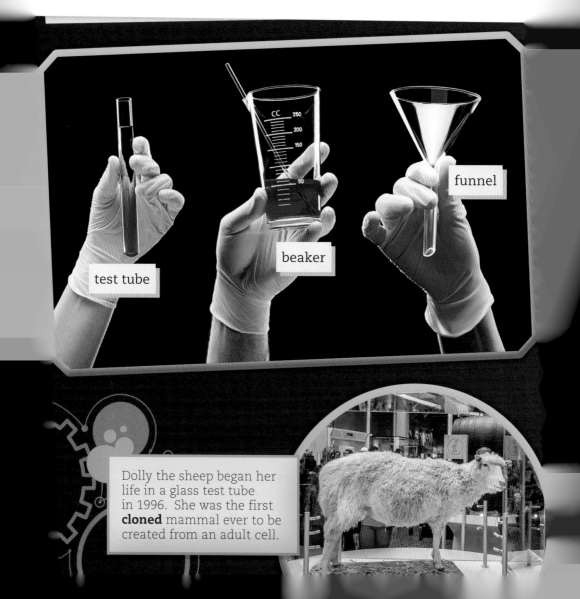

test tube

beaker

funnel

Dolly the sheep began her life in a glass test tube in 1996. She was the first **cloned** mammal ever to be created from an adult cell.

Glass vessels have been used in research for many centuries. Some of those vessels are named after the people who invented them.

Kipp Gas Generator

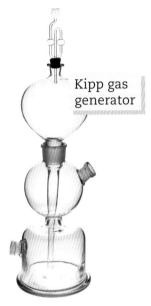

Kipp gas generator

Petrus Kipp was a pharmacist. He lived in the Netherlands. Kipp invented the Kipp gas generator in 1844. The Kipp generator has three glass globes. It creates gas when a cold liquid reacts with a solid material. Scientists often need gas for experiments. The Kipp gas generator is easy to use. It helps scientists make gas when they need it.

Petrus Kipp

Smith Fermentation Tubes

Theobald Smith was an American scientist. He was an expert on bacteria. He wanted to help people stop getting sick from bacteria in water. So, he designed the glass **fermentation** tube. It was used to identify bacteria in drinking water before people drank it. Health departments used his design to make sure water was safe to drink.

Smith fermentation tube

Petri Dish

Julius Petri (YOO-lee-uhs PAY-tree) worked in a lab in Germany in the late 1880s. While there, he designed the Petri (PEE-tree) dish. It is a round, shallow dish with a cover. It is used to grow **microorganisms**, such as bacteria. Petri dishes have clear lids. The lids protect the contents from outside conditions. They also let scientists observe materials with or without microscopes.

Biologist Dorothy Fennel uses a microscope to view specimens in Petri dishes in the early 1940s.

Petri dish

Carrel-Lindbergh Perfusion Pump

In about 1935, Charles Lindbergh and Dr. Alexis Carrel invented a special glass pump. Lindbergh was a famous pilot. He made the first solo nonstop flight across the Atlantic Ocean. But he also knew a lot about **biomechanics**.

The pump pushed **artificial** blood into an organ that had been removed from an animal. The pump led to the invention of the heart-lung machine. A heart-lung machine pumps blood and oxygen when a heart is stopped. It **bypasses** the heart and lungs. Doctors use it when they do open-heart surgery.

This 1938 painting shows Carrel and Lindbergh working on their pump.

ARTS

A Passion for Glass

Kiva Ford is a scientific glassblower. Each flask and test tube he makes is carefully crafted by hand. In his free time, Ford creates works of art out of glass at his studio. He makes goblets and vases. He forms delicate figurines shaped like animals. Ford has a degree in scientific glass technology from Salem Community College.

bottle by Ford

From Lab to Kitchen

Glass was well in use in laboratories in the early 1900s. But it soon spread to other industries including the railroad industry. Railroad workers had a problem. The glass globes they used in signal lanterns often shattered in extreme temperature changes. This was dangerous. Broken signals led to train crashes. William Churchill and George Hollister were scientists at the Corning Glass Works in New York. They wanted to help, so they invented a tough new type of glass called Nonex. It was made of borosilicate. It did not expand or shrink when hot or cold. This made it the perfect material for signal lanterns.

This locomotive relies on Nonex glass signal lanterns.

railroad signal lantern

MATHEMATICS

A Model for Perfect Glass

Smartphones use very thin glass. At first, glassmakers had problems making the glass consistently thin. They asked scientists at Oxford University for help. The scientists developed a mathematical model. The model predicted what glass would do when it was stretched in a furnace. It studied the effects of different temperatures on glass. This helped scientists discover the best temperature to produce perfect glass for smartphones.

Good Housekeeping Magazine ran the first ad for Pyrex in 1915.

The success of Nonex inspired Corning. So, in 1913, Corning hired a scientist named Dr. Jesse Littleton. They challenged him to develop more products the company could make with heat-resistant glass. One day, his wife Bessie showed him one of her casserole dishes that had broken in the oven. She asked her husband whether he could bring home something stronger from work.

Jesse brought home the sawed-off bottoms of two glass jars, and Bessie used them to bake a cake. The containers did not crack in the oven.

Inspired by Bessie's experiments in the kitchen, Jesse invented a stronger glass for Corning. They called the new formula Pyrex® and made a pie plate as their first product. The name comes from a play on the words *pie* and *right* as well as Corning's history of naming their brands with an *x*.

Pyrex Casserole dish

Pyrex ad during World War II

Pyrex products quickly became best sellers. Almost every kitchen in the United States contained a Pyrex casserole dish or bowl. Cooks liked that it was clear. They could watch the food cook inside. Pyrex was also convenient. People could bake, serve, and store food in the same dish. Pyrex did not absorb food odors. It was easy to clean.

Just when cooks thought bakeware could not get any better, Dr. Donald Stookey proved them wrong. He was also a scientist at Corning. While researching the properties of glass, he accidentally overheated a glass plate in a broken furnace. He set the temperature for 600°C (1,112°F). Instead, it heated to 900°C (1,652°F). Stookey was sure the plate would be ruined, but it wasn't! It had turned white, but it had also become shatterproof. Thanks to this furnace **malfunction**, Stookey discovered the technology of glass ceramics. This new formula was used to make CorningWare®, another popular type of cookware.

Stookey's discovery was used for more than baking. Glass ceramics are so strong that the U.S. military puts the material on the noses of guided missiles. It protects missiles from extreme heat. NASA also uses the material to make glass-ceramic nuts and bolts for space shuttles.

Dr. Donald Stookey in 1947

ceramic missile noses

CorningWare casserole dish

CERTIFICATE

The largest measuring cup was created by World Kitchen for Pyrex Brand (USA) in Chicago, Illinois, USA, on 8 March 2015

OFFICIALLY AMAZING

In 2015, World Kitchen made the world's largest measuring cup for Pyrex's 100th anniversary. It is 1.27 meters (4.2 feet) tall and can hold 730 liters (193 gallons).

pyrex SINCE 1915

Innovations in Scientific Glass

Scientists continue to research the properties of glass. They experiment with new ingredients to improve it. They test glass at a range of temperatures.

Scientists want to create glass that is even more resistant to breakage. This will allow more medicines to be shipped safely around the world. Antimicrobial glass is a recent invention. It prevents bacteria from growing on glass. This greatly reduces germs on things, such as smartphones. Scientists have also created an ultra-thin, flexible glass. It is thinner than a human hair. It can be rolled up like a sheet of paper.

Antimicrobial glass stops germs from spreading on things people touch.

This thin, flexible glass can bend without breaking.

When scientists invented a new glass called Chemcor, they tested it by dropping it from the top of a nine-story building!

A scientist inspects a piece of glass.

Scientists will always be able to rely on glass to help them with their research. They will never run out of glass. Why? Glass can be recycled over and over. One thing is clear: glass will continue to play an important role in innovation and discovery!

These glass bottles can be recycled to create new products

GLASS

STEAM CHALLENGE

Define the Problem

Greenhouses are buildings designed to protect vegetables and other plants during cold seasons. They are built using glass or plastic, which trap radiation from the sun and increase the temperature inside the greenhouse. Your task is to design and build an effective greenhouse model for a small plant.

Constraints: Your model must be able to hold a small plant.

Criteria: The internal temperature of your model greenhouse must be higher than the starting temperature after 20 minutes under a light source.

Research and Brainstorm

How do different scientists use glass? How do scientists invent new types of glass to solve problems? What is the most important property of glass? Will the shape of a greenhouse affect the temperature?

Design and Build

Sketch your greenhouse design. What purpose will each part serve? What materials will work best? Build a model.

Test and Improve

Attach a thermometer to the inside of the model and place it under a light source. Record the starting temperature inside the greenhouse. Turn the light on and record the temperature every 5 minutes for 20 minutes. Did it work? How can you improve it? Modify your design and try again.

Reflect and Share

Collect data to figure out whether the shape of a greenhouse changes how effective it is. Which shape is most successful? How do you know? Can you think of another way to test your greenhouse model?

Glossary

artificial—made by people rather than occurring naturally

artisans—people who are skilled at making things by hand

biomechanics—the scientific study of the way the body moves and functions

bypasses—uses another route when the main one is blocked

cloned—created as an exact genetic copy of something else

drafting—the process of producing a technical drawing

essential—necessary and extremely important

fermentation—a chemical change that breaks something down and creates gases

malfunction—failure to function normally

malleable—able to be shaped without breaking or cracking

microorganisms—living things that can only be seen with a microscope

molasses—a thick, sweet, brown liquid made from raw sugar

molds—receptacles in which materials are poured or pressed to make casts

molten—liquefied by heat

nonporous—having a surface without holes, which does not allow liquid or gas to pass through

particles—very small bits or amounts of something

translucent—not completely clear but transparent enough to allow light to pass through

vessels—hollow containers

volatile—likely to change rapidly and unpredictably

Index

Do you want to design scientific instruments?
Here are some tips to get you started.

"As a child, I received a large chemistry set as a gift. I learned a lot about glass and science with that set. If you want to work with scientific instruments, see what vessels you have around your house. Then, find interesting new ways to use them!" —*Jeffery Post, Curator*

"My job as a historian is to find important scientific instruments. These objects document and preserve scientific history. I've learned that you don't always have to be a scientist to work with scientific instruments. Study history or be a science teacher and you can teach people abut the amazing designs behind scientific instruments." —*Steven Turner, Curator*